I
Remember
the
Fallen
Trees

Also by Elizabeth Cook-Lynn

POETRY
Then Badger Said This
Seek the House of Relatives

FICTION
The Power of Horses and Other Stories
From the River's Edge

NON-FICTION
Why I Can't Read Wallace Stegner
*The Politics of Hallowed Ground: Wounded Knee
and the 100 year Struggle for Sovereignty*

I
Remember
the
Fallen
Trees

New *and* Selected Poems
by
Elizabeth Cook-Lynn

EWU
P·R·E·S·S
Eastern Washington University Press
Cheney, Washington 1998

ACKNOWLEDGMENTS

Thanks to the editors of the following journals in which some
of these poems first appeared:

*Pembroke Magazine, Prairie Schooner , Berkeley Poetry Review ,
Wicazo Sa Review, Sun Tracks , The Red Earth, Harper's
Anthology of Twentieth Century Native American Poetry,
Returning the Gift, Unsettling America, The Greenfield Review,
Contact 11,* and *Woyake Kinikiya.*

Library of Congress Cataloging-in-Publication Data
Cook-Lynn, Elizabeth
I remember the fallen trees : poems / by Elizabeth Cook-Lynn
p.   cm.
ISBN 0-910055-45-9 (paper)
ISBN 0-910055-46-7 (cloth)
1. Indians of North America I. Title.
PS3553.05548I14 1998
811' .54 — dc21   98-39668
                    CIP

CONTENTS

For John Roulliard

and all those who have been in the
presence of river gods

PART I

I will stand in my place . . .

NOT EVERYTHING

in the world
had to have a beginning because
some things just always were. Some of
the Sioux say that Inyan, the rock, is the
ancestor of all beings and all things.

Inyan was said to be soft
and without shape
and all-powerful
until he opened himself and bled
and then he became hard
giving some of his power away.

THE MYTHMAKERS

There is a ball game
played with a sacred ball
stuffed with buffalo hair and covered
in the hide of the first relative.

All native peoples know about this sacred ball game.
It is the central myth of the continent.

The Quiches
tell about the Ahup people
who went to play ball
with the Lords of Xibalba
in the region of the dead.

Even the Oglalas
an obscure tribe on the North Plains
through their twentieth century
historian, Nick Black Elk,
spoke reverently
about *tap waka yap*,
the Throwing of the Ball,
a ritual of Lakota/Dakota humanity.

The ball is present at every
important sacred gathering of the people
even today it is painted red and
it has two lines around it
connected with blue dots
at the four quarters.

There is sacredness here
there is sacredness here
there is a sacredness here
there is a sacredness over there

It is said the songs of the
ball players were to become
a dialogue. A narrative
about strength
and the cold
and the heat.
The lead singer
and the others sing
beautiful
incredibly sad
sometimes
songs of elation and power
story-songs
of a people
blacklisted in history
by a new citizenry.

All of us who are serious
about our lives
must look to the arena
where they play the ball game.
We must play it
as we would speak the last word
of slaves and warlords
with sweet pride.

MYTHOLOGY OF THE ETERNAL HOMELANDS

I.

First the Loon Dived

Uncheda, born one hundred years
after the U. S. Constitution was written
in the year that Alexander Graham Bell
invented the telephone

from the beginning a reluctant heiress
to too much land where
exit signs posted by invaders
and tales of solitude in another world
appeared in lucid dreams

We come,
you and I, from the wide, lush
prairie lands and woods of the
northeast to the cramped
bottomlands
at Crow Creek where
the ground is always damp
and reptiles rise from
the weeds to drive for the flesh
of intruders

Uncheda, today your landscape
is light pursuing light
forever a human mirror in memory

unblemished and close to the heart

When I walk to your place
from the flat prairie above, I can
depend on your horses
fraught with the destiny of us all
following me through the dark
discovering my presence

as if by instinct
we pause

Feeling the primal warmth
of their hot breath
I slow down
to let them pass

the darkness seeps into my limbs
nyctalopia and night mist
my only companions I feel
my way, unseeing and alone

Timeless, light
flows only from
the earth and the inner riches
of your snow-capped
years

You never promised me
dark thickets or lightning flashes
of the death journey attached by a mere faint

rainbow to the monsters
of the other side.

II.

So the Muskrat Dived

Though the Agency town
still called "the
heart of the crow"
does nothing to enoble the indifference
of a long and troubled history

we remember how to be born

long-winded, powerful
underwater, the muskrat
carried a fragment of mud in his
claw and we went West
off-hand, dizzy in the moment
and there, alone, we learned to be
Dakotas, slaying the dogs
to be thrown into the great
waters for the spirits

vanishing beneath the surface
to reassure in mortal time
our timelessness

rare evenings

when sleep won't come
we sit in lamplight

we listen to the screech
of the nightowl
and watch for Sputnik

we talk of apostates
and the price we paid.

1880

"Smallpox Used Them Up Winter"

. .   . .

.. ..

.. ..

.. ..

It swept the Great Lakes Tribes
then the Rees and Mandans and
Hidatsas. The Sioux
wrote in their winter counts
that it even went to the Northwest
along the Columbia River
after it finished with them.

1890

Later, when the grave
was fenced, we tied
the sacred red cloths
on the posts.
"I will stand
in my place
until my last day
comes." (Sitanka)

Me ye ksu ya yo.
Me ye ksu ya yo.
When they made the shirts
nothing distracted them
from putting in the
right places
the hanging
eagle feathers.

HISTORY OF UNCHI

—*"Grandchild, I am an old woman
but I have nothing to tell about
myself. I will tell a story."*

They say
that storytellers such as she
hold no knives of blood
no torch of truth
no song of death;
that when the old woman's bones
are wrapped and gone to dust
the sky won't talk and roar
and suns won't sear the fish beneath the sea.

They even say
that her love of what is past
is a terrible thing
hun-he-e-e
what do they know
of glorious songs
and children?

THE BARE FACTS

The spirit lives
when it moves and sings your name
when grandfather and coyote keep warm
together, and lizard gets damp
from the earth, stays fast and hard to kill
when lark flies straight and high to clouds
and you hear buzzard weeping under blankets
when butterfly still talks to women
when ants will fight and die to carry stones
seedlike and shiny from mound to rattle
when we hang by fingernails, remote and hidden
at the ridge of words

the end comes quick
when cricket tells us everything
he knows

TATEKEYA'S EARTH

Looking for the place to cross the creek
I hear a beaver splash and see him
hurry away in spirals of transparency
model busybody on his own
private journey to get home in one piece
alive and well. Like most translators of
these waterways, tributaries to the
great Mni Sosa, he avoided
the great bluffs where I stood
and dropped into low waters
when he heard me intrude.
Predictable, sensible, he
feared the tread of humans,
probably learned he was no match
for those damn builders
whose turbid reservoirs could be heard
upstream for eight hundred miles.

Dusty trails along the tree-lined creek
turn to mud in shaded spots, cow
trails and horse paths lead to the
struggle for meaning of a hard scrabble
life, traditional values of the people
who lived here for thousands of years
displaced as easily as the river chewing
at its banks. Like a Muslim amid
the relics and ruins of any holy city
I weep for Tatekeya's
Earth.

FUNERAL SERMON

— Kudwichacha

Thousands of years ago
they saw an extraordinary sight:
the backbone and ribs
of a creature made of star spirits

they were on their way
and would arrive at the essential place
of naming rituals and sun dances
earth and heaven, rain and wind
would make life worth remembering

they became the
travelers on the Milky Way
and knew the language
of meadowlarks and crows

they were on their way
to a pagan land where relations
between technology and poetry
would conclude in harmless talk
heard on the evening news
or from the hot tubs
on cedar decks of lavish America.

They couldn't know the eight stars
around Gemini* would
disappear

for good
that acolytes
would abandon
landmarks
and legacies

they were on their way
they were on their way

AT MEDICINE CREEK

There are things here that are Siouxan

through slitted eyes I watch layered
clouds driven by the wind like
luckless refuse abandoned to chance.
Just beyond the falls, I'm surprised
by water snakes enjoying the down slide
slipping by as easily as the day.
I think I see the people bathing near places
where old men sat and cleaned the latest catch.
Here the horses splashed toward soft banks
to meet the enemy, their riders
seared against the light of American
Armies and land speculators imposed
on an incredible landscape of hope
to put an end to mythic and unreliable
ages, when dust rose like clouds
driven by the wind.

Here there are things that are Siouxan

a meadowlark sings the songs
that were sung by Sorrel Horse and High Bear
their melodies beyond the lyrics of invaders
who began to follow the Platte River
to the sound of their own endless
clatter and hoofbeats.

MUFFLED THUNDER

in the hills
sounding close and friendly
like a persistent cough
or a talkative lover
who can't leave you alone
definitive, ardent

misted droplets
cold but relenting
wet the windshield
like kinship arbiters

I encounter
the real and imagined
spirits and am annoyed
with them for
appearing in my headlights
like anguished relatives
who know my wounds

DISTANCES

I was writing this poem before I knew how far I had come and
how far, still, I had to go; now, comparing notes taken
then and later, most of the details remembered wrongly,
I find it all so long forgotten. I was nine, reading the parables while
    standing
at the apron of the altar, not in concentration but by rote
and gazing toward the face of Billy Feather, the child Epistle reader,
    a face
even more innocent than mine. We came to convocation, a matter
    of vigil
and community.

The words were not in my heart. Stone valley bushes along
    the creek where the diamond willows grow, sky color light
    against a fishy star in dark waters. That's the real sermon.

After the chokecherries blacken, jackrabbits
    aggregate and blue flowers get off, ambulatory
    on the wind, grass turning mousy and longing for rain
    I come to wonder about disbelief this time of my solitary years.

After walking the dusty roads alone and counting the miles
    all day I see the yellow of my grandmother's dress
    go farther and farther away from the distant reaches of the
    imagined world of parable and Christ's fables; my breath the
    breathed vengeance of a hapless survivor.

I was for a long time convinced that
all this was being said for the first time and
because that was so, distance would not devour me.

THE WAY IT IS

Living here
in the hills, walking
a predestined path
at the edge of the swift water,
the dark of the wind passes time
with birds chatting of good harvest
some sing to remember
some dance to forget

all the old driftings sound the same
as when our ancestors smoked in ritual
the inner bark of red willow

landmarks here of the prairie wildflowers
pay their latest respects as the chilly fall air
catches white coils from my cigarette

things pass and times are gone forever

PART II
witness to the outrage . . .

THERE WAS ONCE a Sisseton woman who could converse with rocks and she was known among her people for this remarkable ability. Once when a young white boy drowned in Lake Kampeska his family called upon this woman as a last resort to locate the body of the unfortunate swimmer. She came from her home in Brown's Valley and walked around the edge of the lake all night, at dawn indicating the place where she said they would find the body. They dragged the lake at that spot and, *ma tuki*, the body was found exactly where the woman said it would be. When they asked her how she was able to perform this incredible act she would only say that the rocks had helped her.

AFTER THE RITUAL

There is, like they say,
"something that moves"
at each of the Four Directions
and the wind
always spoken of
by the holy people
as twelve are its messengers

I'm fit now
now that I'm past my prime
and the ceremony's done
to pay attention as the Badger
hurries across the road
and we drive away
from the Sundance grounds
as light rain wets the windshield and
our small car slips through
the green hills

I can put the questions
of faith to my lips and
wonder aloud about the belief
which caused the old Santee Man
to come to the Council Chambers
in the fall of the year
to ask that the man-made lake
at the bend in the river
be re-named
Dakota Lake

in honor of the people
who had been told many things
by the Unktechies.

REMEMBERING THE SPIRIT AND THE LAND IN THE TIME OF SITTING BULL — *Every People Has a River*

From Appomattox to Wounded Knee
the same white men went about
celebrating their own jury's verdict:
occupy Manila, recapture Geronimo,
invade Cuba,
speaking words of pious
real estate agents: we fill
them with good ideas
so we can take their lands.

Imagine for a moment
the bandit nation holding its breath
in quiet ravines above Grand River
committing "justifiable homicide,"
killing Indians as it would kill
snakes or coyotes or prairie chickens
Imagine the sun driving the horizon shelf
out of sight again
and again
above dirty water
dark water until
it ran crimson over the makeshift bridge
Imagine the dangers even then
A layer of dust would settle
like the sunset curving the earth
in a gesture called the sign of the cross

to make a place for the magic words of pious
poets: we cover the scars of a new nation
staining the glass windows of a moveable river current
with the promises of Paradise.

He saw the flash of a bullet
in the dusk as he walked
not a hundred yards from the Grand River
Imagine there was always the Army
as the empire expanded. There was
always the Army looking into the
impervious shine of the Grand River
reflecting itself in the pious words
of Majors and Generals: they shall see
that there is malice enough in our hearts.
Imagine Indians
hunted like wild beasts along the
sun-drenched river beds
smoke on every horizon
the wounded lying in the bushes
unable to run or regret.

You've got the picture.

KILLDEER IN SNOW

His jeering song connects the wintered Earth
and Sky to fishing grounds of Indians
He imitates the Grandmothers
warns of danger
walks with careful steps
beyond the frozen mud.

Knowing the mutability
of life, he pecks at
bits of pine seeds iced
along the shore.

Feathered, masked in black
his dress of down
appears in dreams to
men who find
the wind-swept stone of black
sought out by
those who shake and
sprinkle herbs.

Time was
when seething waters
rose to meet
his cries.

NEAR SHERIDAN, WYOMING

Buffalo grass, tall and ripening in the
    sun
    drowns out tiny yellow
    flowers
    on spindly stems
and questions old Arapahoes
about how it was
    when they fought
    the Army here
    for thirteen days
    like this one
in ravines
where water rushes down
between the hills
very old
after many centuries
still able to catch the seeds of scrubby pines
and hold them.

(1865 August/September)

GETTING RICH

On promises
we see the silvery band of the river
run on as if waterscapes
tell no stories, reveal no truths

As if there are no scars
no losses

Only rippling waves
and calm
and quiet
into infinity

Later
we cross the bridge
but not before we scrutinize
the cost compose the history
of the world according to
all the pleas of all the Indian priests
we ever knew

Immense distances
hold authority
as we learn
in good conscience
the bitter stories
of broken faith

DRIFTWOOD

The river's down again, my love,
and with the silt and sand
our yesterday is washed away;
we stand in silence here
where souls once touched the shore.

Ask what we did or said
that made us drift away and fade
like trees of pristine worlds
left high and dry.

COLLABORATOR — *Ensuring Domestic Tranquility*

I remember the fallen trees, thin and pale as frost smoke;
and how the wounded river's rippling presence,
witness to the outrage, intentionally or not,
consoled the venal among us. Poor, wind-swept,
the miles and miles of prairie dog-towns
kept our secret. We swam and knew this could become the place
of the unburied, here where the peace treaty
was signed and it was said crimes on both sides
would be forgotten. Buzzard and Old Spotted Eagle
kept watch.

In this mythological Hades descendants
of cow pokes, stirring the tainted water with glimmerous
wands meant to disrupt the questions Indians ask
about the sweet creation of life and death
and meaning take up residence in Buffalo Gap,
the farthest fields. Jedediah Smith was said to tear the hide
from grizzlies, his life inimical to the lives of all living things.

Thin, pale children run
on Cedar Street.

Persistent jets, unseen and ominous
as the shrill of the imagined Red Telephone
whisper in the river's gorge, lapping at the water's edge.
And I walk, intentional or not, amongst
the tourists who are here again
to see the Indians dance.

Forgive me, my children
I barely hear soft raindrops on shrouded drums
of my father and his father and yours.
Periodic, unpredictable, their songs
sway in the gloom
of my forfeiture.

Istohmus waci po
Tuwe yatonwe cin
  Ista nisapa kta
  Ista nisapa kta

. . . OLD WOMAN LOVED TO SING this song of Unktomi's to me when I was a child and the rhythm of it was as unforgettable as the soft, breathless, and ancient sounds her tongue made, her head bent to mine. Such lighthearted sounds, forever in my memory, were in direct polarity with the last songs I remember hearing her sing: the keening, wailing songs of grief at the four-day wake ritualizing the death and burial of her only daughter. The incredible sadness of each sound beginning with and sustaining the high pitch of agony filled me with such sorrow as I had never felt before or since. As each breath ended she began again and again with such great difficulty that I thought she could not go on, and her song seemed to last forever. One of my last mental images of her is how she looked on those days and nights even though she lived many years after that sorrowful event. In this image, she seems to sit on the floor of the small Christian chapel, surrounded by many relatives and friends of the community, her long white hair bound with a black silk scarf. The shiny black cut-beads of her shawl reflect the light from the small kerosene lamp which flickers in one illuminated corner of the room and shimmers with the movements of grief her body makes as she sings. Finally, with the last of her courage, she lets the Catholic priest take the body of her beloved and beautiful daughter and place it in a box and bury it deep inside the darkened earth.

MY GRANDMOTHER'S BURIAL GROUND: PAUL WAHUKEZATININKEYA, JULY 12, 1892

"Words are coins thrown on a table to settle a debt,
a sign that nothing's settled."
—James J. McAuley, "An Irish Bull"

I walked beside the stone
that bore your name and date
and felt the threat of history
give rise to sudden chill, like wind
from an unseen creek. Ancestral bones
lie in anonymity in this New World
except that History called you Christian
and your name
kill-in-war-with-spear
vouched for you.

Grave Paul,
your name as pale as northern Tamarack
in fall, and names of all born then or since
are played like coins
in games of chance. I stand alone
and cast a shadow on the sunken mounds: mute metaphors,
I think, for carelessness of Memory
not then or now for sale or trade.

Never mind, the coins invaders played
which made you play your hand against your will
won't pay the debt. History,
that "counterfeit absurdity"

is no match for Buffalo bones
and dried skins of crows.

ROOM OF GOD AND
DOOR TO HEAVEN
— *A Comment on Indian Missions*

*This poem is dedicated to Eva Lynn who raised
her children in the shadows of this Church of our
Lady of Lourdes, erected by Marquette League at
the West End of the Spokane Indian reservation.
1938.*

Aula dei et porta coeli
open to nothingness
pray for me
for my seeking
Aula Dei et porta coeli

She came to your house
wraithlike
hair and skin of dust
what secrets
in wind and grass
scent your will
to be remote and unforgiving?

Aula dei et porta coeli
open to nothingness
pray for me
for my seeking
Aula dei et porta coeli

Somewhere
there

she almost sang
but now the sound
is
bare
somewhere
there
Aula dei et porta coeli

pray for me
for my seeking
Aula dei et porta coeli.

WITHIN WALKING DISTANCE

—for my widowed mother

You acquiesced when they made you
cut down another elm:

ancient and diseased, they said.
It was an omen.
In your kitchen you wept hot tears.

Now you walk through separate woods
silent, wiping hands on greens
you never saw before.

I am trying to tell you

the porcupine drops his longest quills
in winter. He hides in trees.

And I am waiting for you
on the ground

without much hope.

PART III
in the presence of whiskey traders . . .

IT IS TRUE THAT WOMEN HAVE ALWAYS HAD A VERY HARD TIME. A long time ago when the communal hunts were still going on among the Plains Indians, men rode on powerful horses and were proud providers for their families. And yes, it is true that their lives were hard, also. But, listen, and tell me if you can that a woman's destiny was not one of great difficulty: once, a woman's husband rode out with the others of the tribe on a great buffalo hunt. But luck was not with him that day and his horse tripped. The man broke his neck when he fell and he died instantly. His wife and daughter, for he had no sons, sat and wailed in their grief until the whole tribe had finished the hunt and left them alone with their problems. The old woman placed her husband on a fur robe, tied it securely to the travois and took him back to the camp where a proper burial was held. From that time on they had no man to care for them and they had to take charity from those who felt sorry for them. The daughter often wept in self-pity, and she eventually became a hard-hearted woman, avoided by everyone in the tribe. A woman like this does not have a good life because she believes that richness and joy is in having many children and numerous relatives, and she had neither.

WE STOOD

in the freezing Spearfish
Creek to our ankles; me,
drawing back the line with measured care;
you, holding a chipped-rock spear
poised in the air. It was
the morning after and we never
doubted we would see each other again.

A place like this, you said then,
a place of constant recognition
tells us what is possible.
A place like this, you said then,
is where we may
extend the breath
from an ancient world
into a modern one.

Thinking of this and lost in the
contemplation of my own soul
I could only guess at the
unchangeable
eloquence of that place
in my memory.

MY PREVIOUS LIFE

When I was thirty, my slim bone and muscle
stretching long and nervous like rolls of tissue paper wrapping
hot coals or bloody wounds, I stood in line at the bus stop with
my chu(n)skay, hands caressing his old fishing pole, and my
beautiful daughters, a congregation of wide-eyed souls who trusted
then and now my extemporaneous sermons. We waited to be borne
southward to desert cities where we saw streets flooded with the
annual rainfall in ten-minute lightning bolts. That year was not the
beginning of our exquisite bond but its memory stretches like deer hide
on a drum, to make a sacred resound. In the night our luggage got off
in Denver and we beamed on through the darkness stripped of
toothbrushes and extra underwear vulnerable as naked
roses in the fall. In less time than it takes to tell of the fear and pain
of a vision dying, no secret so alive as that of a family unable to
complete itself, we U-Hauled it back to Crow Creek where we stood
in chilly mists like trees yellowed and spent or old folks
at the care center singing tired songs of the past. Out
of the wind and safe. We were home again where silences
toward failed women of bad marriages imprison the future
of their children. We lighted candles in a church that
didn't want us and I took a job giving English assignments
to battered men who claimed they couldn't "write worth shit,"
fists swollen and at the ready. Eventually, we drove our
aging Pontiac to a college town which led us through days
designed by racist professors and disciplines that deserved to
be blown up, splintered and charred. In that place, still warm
from regular paychecks and full tables we grew to know that
those who suffer loneliness don't always learn to despise
themselves if their bellies are full.

I look back on that thirtieth year as a year of departure, everything before that the trappings of a previous life of false hope, everything after an acknowledgment that nothing matters except the love of those who love you.

FREQUENTLY ASKED QUESTIONS

I'm always asked about the latest dance
by those who think I need
to feel secure
and then I try the steps
and make believe these fingers don't belong
to wet and clammy hands.
They say
it's good to gorge the bellies at the feast
we speak of in contemporary terms.

I'm never asked by those who think
the feast is now or soon
why shaking gourds I know have lain in dust
for years brings out the best
in me.

I think
they think
it is most certainly
an act of faith to seem unripe.

NOVEMBER DAY

—for Mary

So dry we couldn't weep or curse
we scraped across the autumn wind
and listened to the moan of air
which snuffed the warmth from cozy roots

Like hollow, nameless leaves
we disappeared
borne swiftly off by chilly gusts
Our time was past

Immutably, I think of this
on all November days
and more

ALL THINGS WILL PASS

You brought me bone
out of eyes of grief
some things just look, I said
no more
no less.

After that you brought me feathers
On your back
And cried into the sky.

The rest went bad
And the meadowlark declared us dead.

WHEN YOU TALK OF THIS

Wine-puffed
lesions
below the eyes
won't tell what dreams are

> *Christ, I'm*
> *sick!*
> *Oh, Christ,*
> *I'm sick!*

Roused from
acquiescent
torpor
his gestures seem bizarre
raking garbage
from shiny tins

Don't say
he didn't remember
he'd shot his brother
and why
Say:
his children loved him
and his wife
was a good and faithful woman.

SIMILE

Meditation
constantly practiced
under endless overcast skies
feels the sting
of sensing
but never knowing
like a woman walking
barefoot
with her lover
through the woods where
pine needles lie down
in layers, stiffened
by the sun.
Eventually
she stretches her arms
expectedly
vividly
and begins the dance.

KEYA PI

I.

"I stood
watching the strays,"
he said.
"And among them
was a human being."

II.

The girl,
lila wiyan waste,
wife of Walking Bear,
disappeared
while they were moving to a new camp.
And she never did come back.
There was no need.
For her to come back, I mean,
since the two children
lived pleasantly
with relatives
and the husband
adjusted to his loss.

Yet
something
made him
join the chase
and they trapped
the horses in a small area.

She was swift.
And beautiful.

She tried to get away
and refused to eat.

So, Walking Bear
cut the rope
and let her go her way,

III.

Again, they chased the
stray herd
and surrounded them
when suddenly
a black bird
flew up
and sat on a cliff
stealthily
watching them.

IV.

Later
he would say
she was lured away by them.

But,
what could you expect?

She was Kiowa, anyway.

A SUMMER VISIT

— to my mother at the Maryhouse

Her wide window overlooks
green gardens, an empty tennis court
and a white-draped figure
of the Virgin Mary,
Mother of God. Her face slams shut
shattering the serene still-life
reminding me that I am
the religious one. Not she. And, besides,
she says, she does not belong here with her
senile neighbors.

She won't be seen using a walking stick
so I push her in a wheelchair
into the hot wind, her sparse white hairs
blowing like cotton gauze across
her broken gaze. Like pools of grieving idle light
her darkened eyes search my face and
scorn the fear she sees in me. She
refuses to go downstairs
where dinner is served
because they will look at her.

Accusing. Her eyes look through me
when I ask her to come and
live with me. Lord hear my prayer.
Lord hear my prayer. Lord hear
my prayer.

MY FLIGHT

How can I know
what keeps me disengaged, fleeing
for my life? An emigré, I never meant
to stay here routinely professing
in this wordless, sad New World.
Darkly, I meet others
in the hallway: those who
survive our lives
resist the market mentality
and believe the saving
of baby seals
is a reinvention
of Humanism.

I dreamed I locked the door
and left.

See you later!

No roadsigns point me
in the right direction. When
Oyate gather to sing the songs
that Little Horse sang
I will be there.

THE LAST WORD

You'll never play Paganini's guitar
I said as I left you sitting
your chin on the
greasy table
you're no one to
lift a fine glass with
and if I see you at Antelope next summer
I'll walk by as if I never knew you.

AFTER A LONG WINTER

Between the touching hills, a shield of pine,
yellow birds glisten, hiding out behind
the gesture of a broken wing, they
claim the song from god knows where
and the blue and nameless skies are warmed. No wind.
The pause we shared exquisitely absorbs
the wound and deer are dark and silent miles away.

Without the presence of the wind, no melody
of sacred lies, one tends to put aside
the silly words one said and heard. And now forgot.
The everlasting chant of us, a singing pair,
will echo from the hills and memory will
glare golden in the sun.

WIDOWHOOD

I.

At death's best hour
she waved away
those
who might have cared
unloved matriarch
she called herself
abandoned and unlucky
survivor.

Swaying in the faded summer breeze
the walls creaked. A door
shifted. Her wail
slipped from its place
like the Chief's blanket
from her thin shoulders
as she bent to peer
slow and sodden
into his bleak, chill
years.
Stay.
Stay.

II.

She thought she remembered herself
as a graceful, glimmering
wisp, not this
weathered wooden yard fence

paint peeling, the cornerposts sagging
into barriers of intolerable

waiting, waiting
keeping things in or out
refusing to give way
to the traffic
the coming and going.

III.

Elsewhere, nocturnal insects
grew silent. An Indian
priest plucked his medicine
and held it in his palm

contemplative
elegaic

what had changed the world?

CONTRADICTION

As one who does not mind
the transitory touch that
makes woman-song so breathless, blind,
she hears the wolves at night
prophetically: put them behind,
the legends we have found
care not a bit
go make a night of it!

She wonders why you dress your eyes
in pulsing shades of Muscatel,
why wailing songs of what-the-hell
make essences to eulogize.

Sometimes she squints against the sun
that is your face, no place to run.

Yet, every time the beavers judge
the depth of dams for winter's grudge
she knows the risk
that's in the ice
when women throw down bundles.

SPIDER AS SHE USED TO BE

1.

Swiftly, innocently,
the primordial

spider weaves her way
into cracks of ceiling logs

a moment ahead of the wasp

I stack the fireplace tamarack
and resolve to be more

cunning.

2.

The woman who lived here
before me

now silent
traceless as the wind

knew how to keep a fire

she walked these steep hills
in winter, scouting for firewood

past the grease brush
beyond a loosened fence

and when her children grew
she refused to send them to school

jcalous, rcbuked in a quarrel
with a second wife

she left her husband
and set out

to be with her relatives.

In those times
slaves were still being

brought to America
and Alfred Lord Tennyson

was writing
"Break, Break, Break"

America! America!

Alone
the woman who lived here

before me

cried for fire

her grandfathers went part of the way
with her and when lightning

struck a tree
she dried the meat

they had provided. At nightfall
they pushed her around in the dark

and let her go.

Her relatives danced upon her grief.[*]

3.

Her fathers remained where they had fallen
and the Indian killers

delivered to civil authorities

in Bismarck

escaped.[†]

4.

Like the primordial spider

she webbed her way into ceiling logs

managing to look back at the

space of human order, her
old, yet innocent eyes

assuming that hidden gods

would rescue her.

5.

Furious, vengeful, I stir
charred tamarack

ashes of the dead

I open the damper to clear the soot

"Another time," I promise
the woman who lived here

before me. "Another time."

It is my duty to keep the fire.

I silently promise
the woman who lived here
before me that in this

burnt-out twentieth century
the flame won't flicker and out.

6.

Trying to rethink what is significant
I watch with great attentiveness

as the familiar spider
makes her way

from underground chambers
of ancient life

to the heat of ceiling logs.

It is here

in the presence of whiskey traders
that the risk is

glittering and golden.

PART IV
we may pretend . . .

WHEN THE DAKOTAPI REALLY LIVED AS THEY WISHED, they thought it important to possess a significant tattoo mark. This enabled them to identify themselves for the grandmothers who stood on the ghost road entering the spirit world asking *"Mitakoja* (grandchild), where is your tattoo?" If the Dakotah could not show them his mark, they pushed that one down an abyss and he never reached the spirit land.

THE LAST REMARKABLE MAN

Old Hunka* of the people
your scarred breast
grows soft and translucent
in blue-gray photos on the wall
in oval frames, hidden under dust
A man to be remembered
your ancient tongue warms men
of fewer years and lesser view
You tell of those who came, too busy fingering lives
with paper to know what they can't know

> They liked the oratory but thought the case was
> hopeless:
> go home, old Benno, it loses something in
> translation
> drink the wind and darken scraps of meat and bone

stars won't rise in dreams again
Heads bent to clay-packed earth,
we smoke Bull Durham for bark of cedar
but know: in council, talk's not cheap
nor careless in its passing. The feast
begins with your after-vision, ahead of its time

> We speak of you in pre-poetic ritual.

THE WORLD HE LIVED IN

was like some vast museum with rock walls
where he was safe from the torrents of rain
but lifeless as artifact,
cellophaned, preserved. He put
great faith in the holy men who sang
to hailstones because, he said, there
are four posts holding up the Earth
and four beavers busily gnawing
at each.

He lived in the museum of rock walls,
paleolithic and alone, habitually ascetic,
questioning the reliability
of messages from curators
only recently revealed. Fraudulent.
Capricious. Their imaginary
lives and deaths encompassed his misery.

Eventually he became the man who walked
into the day, following a ditch
along a country road so luminous
he couldn't find his way home. Heat from
the glossy rocks on this isolated country road
marred his forehead and cheek and when the others
found him he was too weak to breathe,
              supine and covered with dust.

GRANDFATHER AT THE INDIAN HEALTH CLINIC

It's cold at last and cautious winds creep
softly into coves along the river bank. At my insistence
he wears his denim cowboy coat high on his neck; averse to
an unceremonious world, he follows me through
hallways pushing down the easy rage he always has
with me, a youngest child, and smiles.
This morning the lodge is closed to the dance
and he reminds me these are not men who raise the bag above
painted marks; for the young
intern from New Jersey he bares his chest
but keeps a scarf tied on his steel-gray braids
and thinks of days that have no turning: he wore
yellow chaps and went as far as Canada to ride
Mad Dog and then came home to drive the Greenwood Woman's
cattle to his brother's place.
Two hundred miles
along the timber line
the trees were bright
he turned his hat brim down in summer rain.

Now winter's here, he says, in this white lighted place
where lives are sometimes saved by
throwing blankets over spaces where the leaves are brushed away
and giving brilliant gourd-shell rattles
to everyone who comes.

SOME OF MY BEST FRIENDS

To get things straight
must your eyes see what my eyes see?
The Marabar Caves as Womb?
Bear Butte as Vision?

I have a funny feeling
that the universal spread of myths of men
is a put-up job, flyspecked and empty
that alliance will jam and thaw and flood
and Woolf will out.

We have walked away from history
and dallied with a repetition of things
to the end of the bar and booze.
Like a time bomb it ticks as rapidly
for White Hawk as for Little Crow
or me.

A LONG WAY

We seldom mentioned him,
my favorite uncle,
but he came back every now and then
his smile touched
by his captivity.
For me
he sang the unreal songs
and mended the wind.

Remembering the old woman
who threw the ball
out of the tipi four times
and saw it come back as something else
they said, cautiously,
"you're back . . . ?"
But he said, "no . . . I'm a long way
from back. . . ."

I sat and cried
that the night was full of darkness
so he told me about the sunflower
springing from Sun Gazer's burial mound
to turn its face
at different times of the day
everlastingly
toward the sun.

A POET'S LAMENT — *Concerning the Massacre of Lakotas at Wounded Knee*

All things considered, they said,
Crow Dog should be removed.
With Sitting Bull dead
it was easier said.

And so the sadly shrouded songs of poets,
ash-yellowed, crisp with age
arise from drums to mark in fours
three times the sacred ways
that prayers are listened for; an infant girl stares
past the night, her beaded cap of buckskin brightens
Stars and Stripes that pierce
her mother's breast; Hokshila, innocent
as snow birds, tells of Ate's blood as red as plumes
that later decorate the posts of death.

"Avenge the slaughtered saints," beg mad-eyed
poets everywhere as if the "bloody Piemontese" are real
and really care for liberty of creed; the blind
who lead the blind will consecreate the Deed, indeed!

All things considered, they said,
Crow Dog should be removed.
With Sitting Bull dead
it was easier said.

AT DAWN, SITTING IN MY FATHER'S HOUSE

I.

        I sit quietly
in the dawn; a small house in the Missouri breaks.
A coyote pads toward the timber, sleepless as I,
guilty and watchful. The birds are commenting on his
passing. Young Indian riders are here to take the old
man's gelding to be used as a pick-up horse at the
community rodeo. I feel fine. The sun rises.

II.

        I see him
from the window; almost blind, he is on his hands and
knees gardening in the pale glow. A hawk, an early riser,
hoping for a careless rodent or blow snake, hangs in the wind
current just behind the house: a signal the world is
right with itself.

        I see him
from the days no longer new chopping at the hard-packed
earth, heedless of the dismal rain. I hold the seeds
cupped in my hands.

III.

        The sunrise nearly finished
the old man's dog stays here waiting, waiting, whines
at the door, lonesome for the gentle man who lived here. I
get up and go outside and we take the small footpath to the
flat prairie above. We may pretend.

PROFILE OF THE SUN AND MY
AGING FATHER

In that moment of time
between Creation and Death
when Sun streaks heat
in layers of red and purple
then fades behind gray shields
on frozen December dawns,
I see your face
turned sideways
dark against the sky,
I trace the lines
and grieve that Earth lies
dormant
wise
and inaccessible.

In the dead of winter
hawks return to steal the words
you might have said
and fly them into shadows of the sun
to reaffirm the Plains' long daytime.

HOW THE MAN BROKE HORSES

He rode the familiar plain toward
Swiftwater, dark and seething, murderous
in the heat and dust of a hundred years
of Dakota hunters outwitting their luckless prey. The sleek
blooded roan beneath him needed fire, foamed wet
at the mouth from chomping at the bit, prancing witness
to a day's hard night. Not even a wedge of light
from ravines and side roads shadowed the hold
angry gods had on him.

From the other men's wives he slept with
while mastering moonscape and prairie wilds
not a dime's worth of thanks
for his lust. His beauty was a tribute
to this ancient tribe, pipedream now
from the lonely and triumphant cannibals.

Ovation was not his thing, no need for
applause, no Orphic devotion to the oldest principles.
The civic-minded better step out of the way
When he was young he loved Big Pipe's place
and spoke the names of those
who knew what it was like
to ride a horse down. Reverently.

A WOMAN'S OLD AGE

She had come to the time of her life
when she had to struggle
to defend her innocence;
cynicism came much too easily
like handsome birds of prey moving in
stealthily, disgorging tufts of bone,
eliminating frightened and watchful rodents.

In this silence
in this cave of bound things
she and the man she has lived with
off and on for fifty years
have never learned the darkness
of each other's souls because
everything has stood for
high and mighty values.

It is only from the casual things
that you can walk away.

PART V
children of the prarie hawks . . .

BY THE TIME the United States entered World War I, Sioux Indians had been living on reservations for a lifetime, and even though unimaginable changes had been endured, the soul of the tribe continued in the imagination to be inherent in Maka, the Earth.

JOURNEY

I.

Dream

    Wet, sickly
smells of cattle-yard silage fill the prairie air
far beyond the timber; the nightmare only just
begun, a blackened cloud moves past the sun
to dim the river's glare, a malady of modern times.

II.

Memory

Dancers with cane whistles,
the prairie's wise and knowing kinsmen.
They trimmed their deer skins
in red down feathers,
made drumsticks from the gray grouse,
metaphorically speaking, and knocked on doors
which faced the east.
Dancers with cane whistles
born under the sign of hollow stems,
after earth and air and fire and water
you conjure faith to clear the day.
Stunningly, blessedly, you pierce the sky
with sound so clear each winged creature soars.

In my mind, Grandmothers, those old partisans of faith
who long for shrill and glowing rituals of the past

recall the times they went on long communal
buffalo hunts; because of this they tell the
lithe and lissome daughters

> look for men who know the sacred ways
> look for men who wear the white-striped quill
> look for dancers with cane whistles
> and seek the house of relatives to stay the night.

III.

Sacristans

This journey through another world, beyond bad dreams
beyond the memories of a murdered generation,
mapped in their captivity by bare survivors
makes sacristans of us all.

The old ones go our bail, we oblate preachers of our tribes.
Be careful, they say, don't hock the beads of
kinship agonies; the moire-effect of unfamiliar hymns
upon our own, a change in pitch or shrillness of the voice
transforms the waves of song to words of poetry or prose
and makes distinctions
no one recognizes.
Surrounded and absorbed, we tread like Etruscans
at the edge of useless law; we pray
to the giver of prayers, we give the cane whistle
in ceremony, we swing the heavy silver chain
of incense burners. Migrations make
new citizens of Rome.

REVISION

—for your grandfather

Looking back
A funny kind of whirlwind
Goosed and rolled and told
Of enormous blunders.

The mongrel dog choked on his life
Spiders turned their backs on webs
The Four Thunders made you sad
And only when you made me listen
Was I alive.

GOING HOME

Those roads of hard packed earth, streaked with the familiarity
of noon, sag where heat-struck reptiles smear their unborn

and dogs live out the defeat of silence

soft, warm, old women ignore my thin embrace

Those roads to the wombs of the sovereign tribes, motherlands to
starvelings born again by taking the veil, entering religious orders
and reciting cantos to the Holy Ghost

those roads that pass the recent profligate Missouri, process server
for Jefferson who only wanted to replace the Indian-head nickel
and set up residence anywhere in the darkness of the cave

those roads that pass the graveyards
those roads that pass the severely wounded

come, finally, to the place where I grew up by the campfires
snuffed out by colonials who brought with them
the frame houses with closed porches

jogging suits

Black Hills Power and Light

Valedictorians and Pied Pipers of every order.

MAKE BELIEVE

*"When they told him he was to become an American, they
said it this way: 'My son, what you have to do is to take
care of the white people, and try to raise two or three
streaks of grass.'"*
— Smutty Bear, the Yankton Tribe, 1856.

Curtain rises!
The ceaseless rolling of a rock
to the top of the mountain, burdened, colonized,
like the slaves of another age
to live by the laws other than one's own.
Doomed! Like Greek
heroic figures created by the epic poet Homer,
Sisyphus was probably condemned by the Gods
though opinions differ on this,
because he loved the world
too passionately!

At the foot of the mountain
he will always find his burden again
and forever labor in the underworld. The torment
is tolerable only as it is imagined, appearing
in the mythological consciousness
of colonials. It offers the possibility
of a standing-room-only curtain call.
I'm sad to say, here, where the air is clear
the play which deserves no re-runs
is sold out.

THE JAMES BAY CREE

and their neighbors, the Naskapi
Indians, and the Eastern Inuit
join in the indigenous resistence
to the idea that a river
and its people can be
destroyed
without conscience:

> *"this monument*
> *is erected in memory*
> *of our Cree Ancestors who,*
> *having lived off this land*
> *for thousands of years,*
> *now rest under the waters*
> *of the reservoirs*
> *of Le Grande Complexe*
>
> *I know that my redeemer liveth*
> *and that he shall stand*
> *at the latter day*
> *upon the earth." (Job 19-25)*

GHAZAL #1

One of these days we'll all be hiding out like treed
porcupines staring into the yellow glare of the flashlight.

Workers in gold and silver, first, then uranium, have become
the illuminators of sacred ideas who now people the world.

Summer rain shimmers wet circles on tailing ponds so
lethal barren birds fall out of the sky.

It all began, perhaps, in a search for Byzantium,
that symbol of a world of artifice and timelessness.

Poets, I say there's nothing wrong with the decay and
death of the natural and sensual world.

GHAZAL #2

Whether well and accurately or poorly and falsely, tribal Boswells
and Stracheys discover their histories. Listening. Rising.

Narratives of the men and women of the North Plains rose from the
flatness of the land surrounding them. And from their poetry.

We stumbled toward the door, opened it, and white fog rolled in around
our feet. After that, we guarded the sealed openings of the room.

Clouds, too, added phrases which fell upon the land but only
for an instant and when their shadows lifted, the sun blazed.

A bull elk, alone and separated from the herd, sauntering
stiff-kneed toward the river, whistled.

GHAZAL #3

The Missouri Breaks, lying between the uplands and river bottoms,
become the sacrifice area for the hydro-power dams.

He grew up listening to the Wahpekute singers and when he was
down on his luck he expected to hear their songs, essential and true.

Corn stalks, draped and browned, brittle shrouds, stand mute,
spent; sentinels of Fall as the next to the last dance is held.

"My old mother," he says, "doesn't know me. 'A man came to see
me yesterday', she says of my visit, 'and he was from Montana.'"

A Dakotah man did not take a second wife because he was
tired of the first; that was not the way of a good Dakotah.

A MOMENT — *Standing in the Post*
Office to Keep Warm, Rapid City, South
Dakota

Silently, the day so sunless spirits weep,
a man I used to know stared out at me with eyes
of quintessential age reminding me
our lives are hard; I wave. He smiles.
And both of us still see the bridge we crossed
when we were children
of prairie hawks.

TO WHOMEVER ONE CALLS
WHENEVER ONE HAS A QUARTER

I drive many miles through towns where the only
brick building is the Liquor Store. I pass by
familiar land shapes so spectacular they
never fail to turn my head, to places where
white men, selfish to the bone, vague and secretive
and loud, name themselves as nationalists whose
balance of trade is in the red, from Sundance to
Newcastle, where Indian landlords
are on a par with white-trash drifters
and wife-beaters.

An antelope stands in the
mid-morning sun looking like he has
a bad stomach.

In a canyon a dog barks.

Too many of us still don't get the message.

My radio is playing Carlos Barbosa-Lima's
version of Classical Gas and I worry
that the pact we made in order to
save ourselves marks us survivors of the wasteful dead,
the distant sun mourning our lack of resolve,
the wind dancing on telephone lines
hooked up to oblivion.

JESUS SAVES OR DON'T ASK ME TO
JOIN AA AND BE A FOOL

I told you once, there is a trend
toward sounding senseless, as it were,
I think I'll sing a forty-nine* instead.

The second, third and fourth descend,
I should be sober, to be sure,
I told you once there is a trend

toward seeking vision, faceless end
but fools are fools, we all concur,
I think I'll sing a forty-nine instead

The question is: Do you defend,
bear witness to a false quick-cure?
I told you once there is a trend

and you're as sick as I, my friend,
though songs of Passion hearts bestir
I think I'll sing a forty-nine instead.

You want for me what's in your head
but what's in mine I must prefer,
I told you once there is a trend
I think I'll sing a forty-nine instead.

AN INDIAN RESERVATION SONG

Who stole Indian land today? I want
to know, being Indian myself and
concerned about History and the next generation.
Who stole Indian land today?
Not Custer. Not gold miners. Not pioneers, long dead.
      Would you believe
        the senator who needs the votes,
        a judge who can't say "no"?
Who stole Indian land today? Was it Mr. Watt?
or Mr. Pick and Mr. Sloan, those
architects who say "our Indians,"
change important rivers people live by
and browse the Wall Street Journal on the side?
Who stole Indian land today?
      Would you believe
        astute members of the Bar, numerous as flies,
        more intimate with tribes than husbands and wives:
        have lakes and mountains named for themselves
        dance at the ground-hog time, pretend
        the "wanna-be" connection?
Who stole Indian land today?
      Well,
      would you believe
      some skin who knows the bureaucratic
      ropes and wants to retire from
      one cushy job to another?

TRESPASS

Wind moans off prairie hills. Hang on.
Tinpsina blooms whitish blue,
crisp in the hard black earth,
Wind moans off prairie hills. Hang on.
> Just across the creek and up the
> hill from Big Pipe's place, the
> CCC camp bustled, men chipped
> at rocks for the dam's bedding.
> Indians were hired there for
> pick-and-shovel jobs and some
> for driving trucks. White men
> married to tribal women also
> worked there as foremen and they
> ate their boxed lunches in separate
> and isolated places, looking
> persistently stern and important.
Wind moans off prairie hills. Hang on.
Tinpsina blooms whitish blue,
crisp in the hard black earth.
Wind moans off prairie hills. Hang on.
> Big Pipe owned the access road
> and sat astride his horse with a
> loaded SHARPS in his hand
> and watched the horse-backs, the 1932
> Fords, and the team-drawn wagons
> cross the creek at his place each
> morning and evening.
Wind moans off prairie hills. Hang on.
Chokecherry blooms sweet and white,

abundant in green leaves.
Wind moans off prairie hills. Hang on.
> After a long while Big Pipe asked them
> aloud, "What are the implications of
> your presence here? Do you believe that
> you are on white man's land and that you
> have a right to do his harvesting?" Confident,
> vivid, in full glare of his own
> individuality, he questioned: "Do you
> think me uncooperative? Mad? Arrogant
> or sad? Do you think me dumb? Without
> language or grace?"

Wind moans off prairie hills. Hang on.
Chokecherry blooms sweet and white,
abundant in green leaves.
Wind moans off prairie hills. Hang on.
> O my brothers, this is the place
> where I as a young boy swam with
> the otter; and I will teach my grandsons
> here, in this place, where I as a young
> boy swam with the otter.

Wind moans off prairie hills. Hang on.

A POEM FOR MY EX-BROTHER-IN-LAW

He slit the yellow belly of a rattler
to show the children how the ancient ones were born
and said, "They're survivors." Nothing dies,
he believes, not even the deserving.

He put his house in the shadow
of Thunder Butte and fathered six children
one right after the other.
Diligent, ever factional, we languished
in despair at the D & E
where Long Tall Sally tended bar
and he talked to me of personal histories gone sour.

MOUNT RUSHMORE

Owls hang in the night air
between the visages of Washington, Lincoln,
the Rough Rider, and Jefferson; coyotes
mourn the theft of sacred ground.

A cenotaph becomes the tourist temple
of the profane.

FOR THE INDIANS IN THE MINT BAR
WHO ROBBED THE JOINT AND
HEADED FOR THE STATELINE
BY CALLING A CAB

In a world where all the villains
cruise the night while mincing words
the two sit silent, stroking glass on glass,
keeping stories warm, untold, and real.
Days and nights of grief spin out
of flickering juke-boxes to
keen of loss of those who used to care.

No mourners, they, who drink and watch the
fools play games in tough country.
They silently applaud
the stiff-haired Navajo
who wants his money guaranteed.

A perfect pair, they dramatize the comic scenes
of non-translatable plays.

PART VI
in the company of river gods . . .

THE BLEAK TRUTH IS

the old man knew many
stories about the river
he told them only when he was angry

when they wouldn't do what he asked
he would say to them in Indian, "you must meet me
by the river seven days from now"

he would frighten them with his look
and they would be compelled to go after him

as for myself, I have seen the butte
where the old man now
sleeps but I do not walk on it
it is a place out in the prairie where the grass grows
and the wind remembers his English idioms: "I don't like people
who go behind the bush and beat around."

THE COVE

was a quiet place
hidden from above by an overhang
of oaks and leafy bushes
where my uncles
stripped naked
swam with powerful strokes
to the other side of the darkened river
then stood for several long moments
in the shaded strip of beach
before returning

there was no hurry, no talking
no struggle to win or be the best
I call from memory the water sounds
of their familial communion
their poised hands and flashing arms
reaching toward the browning shore

once, when I was no longer a child
I went there to stare at the grey depths
and witness the alien banks
and shout their names

THEY SEEMED

to come from the depths and
looking at the phenomenon with great interest
the old Santee remembered the stories about
the remarkable unktechies who
at the beginning of time
ripped off first one arm
and then the other and flung them
into the water. One was
a female figure and the other a male.
They taught the Dakotas what they needed to know
about religion and, it was said, the female subsequently
went deep into the earth, herself.
"She is still there," the old women will tell you,
"waiting and listening for the prayers of Indians.
She is listening
to hear
the drums
of Indians."

DELUGE

I.

Look at the disorder
the leaves and vines torn from swaying trees
dissolute and needy, scattered as signs
of the presence of water gods. Rain, telling stories
of all the floods the world has ever known, splashes
the deck outside my window, blatant intercessor

inconvenient as a family quarrel at suppertime
bringing with it a seriousness that chastens my selfish
thoughts about a dark past when I, licking bad wounds

like stinging salty spray, couldn't tell the difference
between depression and despair. A bad marriage
gasped its last breath begging us to come to terms with
ourselves, to say what was to go on between past and present
and future lives. Which is why we sloshed barefoot across
the flooded paths to the other side. Like old outcasts

inconsiderately destined to wed the green and grateful
bereaved. Rain scattering on rooftops commits itself to
rushing forces beyond our control and reminds us
that when water, like fire, is stolen by the gods
it is only the Wind that comes to the rescue.

II.

Look across the river to the place we hunted grouse. That
place where you told me: you'll be sorry. Wind and Rain
incriminate the past and manage to perpetuate
the personal storm. Twenty years on there is still the
tardy bridgroom who makes excuses. But none for me.
Without answers to questions of what went wrong and why
only the river gods will tell you what you can expect.

AN ACADEMIC POEM FOR INDIAN DISSENTERS

I don't speak of Kunstler or AIM
or Oppression of Women's Rights or Yellow Thunder Camp;
just inter-library loans and grade point averages
and campus Cold Wars. Colonial Academia has
turned my grief into anything but
the Uprising which is deep in my heritage.

I've been in this place too long, the Irish poet says
and I know he means me; all the wrong turns
succeed, the right ones diminished
by Quarterlies, rigorously competitive,
sworn in for Promotion.
Indian Preference aside, slumlords
of the disciplines rent out our kind
to the corrupt local machines and finance
the status quo professing
"Consent of the Governed" and Civil Liberties.

Architects of the old fascism
pay me to be obedient and subservient
on behalf of the untouchables
and whenever I think I have no blue print
for political remedy
I reach for paper and pen.

PART VII
no magic sets you free . . .

LITERAL HISTORY HAS HAD ITS SPECIAL WAY
of describing the tragedy of the American Indian, and it has
taken on a substance of its own as all histories do. In one sense
that kind of history is valid and real, of course, but in another it is
a cruel distortion, like concentrating in sorrow on the traceless
disappearance of winter snow beneath the sun without the telling
of nourishment for early spring fertility. This distortion comes
about, I believe, because the traditions of literal men suffer a
weakness, a flaw, a silence which makes them seem deaf. Literal
history, you see, has no sound. Yet, sound, however faint and
fickle, is essential to identity and survival. There are many
ancient stories told in various contexts throughout all oral
cultures emphasizing the importance of sound. This is one told
by the Sioux:

> Swan was a young Sioux boy who liked to study
> tracks and signs and other things a warrior
> must know to become famous as a scout in his
> tribe. His interests became known to the
> headman who then asked him to scout the location
> of an enemy and bring back news of their strength
> both in horses and warriors.
>
> Swan traveled without stopping for food and he
> watched every sign in the air, on the ground and
> in the bushes and trees. At nightfall he was
> very tired and so he set his tipi and started to
> prepare his arrows for whatever might befall him
> in enemy country.

Sitting by his fire, Swan carefully ground the
edges of an arrow between two flat stones to make
the point sharper. He was so intent upon his work
that when an owl in the tree over his tent softly
spoke, "who-oo-o, wh-oo-o-o," it seemed so close
that he was startled and he dropped his arrow. As
he bent over to pick up the arrow, his eyes rested
on the surface of a bowl of water he had placed near
the fire when he was getting his evening meal. He
saw reflected in the water the face of an enemy
looking down at him through the smoke hole in
the top of the tipi.

Showing no sign of having heard the owl nor of
having seen the enemy face, Swan continued to
sharpen his bow, turning this way and that, sighting
its accuracy. Then with a quick twist of the wrist, he
shot an arrow straight up through the face looking
down at him. The enemy scout fell over dead.

In native cultures the story is told with varying events and settings but
the message is essentially the same. The "who-oo-o" of the owl is a
significant statement, however ambiguous and, if it is your belief that
creative and spontaneous acts can bridge the gap between what is
known and what is not, the gathering of sensory data available to you
gives the process of language and, ultimately, history, a credence
scorned by literal men. The response to sound is evident in all Sioux
art forms, and in historical recitation it is profound and complete.
Accountably, then, Swan's history remained his own and when he
returned to the camp and told his people that the owl spoke to him,
they knew it to be true.

CITY GAMES OF LIFE AND DEATH
— *Walking the Mission District of*
San Francisco

I can see why Indians come here
and never go home again
vast splendorous glittering glass panes
reflect someone else's shadow
and swift cars people every curve
slanting streets which are the cemeteries
of conscious thought numbly forecast that tomorrow
the wolves will finally come. But
no one hears beyond the primal call of the flesh.
Thus, winos and scholars and horsemen
and gods gathered in for the
astonishing ritual go for the stars. For them there is no
homeland and they are doomed. They lead each other
in the heavenly dance. Colonial revivalists on
city reservations hum, again, the Flood Control Act
of 1936 in waist-deep monotone
and say, finally,
"they have changed their ways."

A PROSE POEM — *In Honor of the Rise of the American Indian Movement*

Sacred and religious in form, a man with red-wrapped braids offering the secrets of self-sacrifice and regeneration appeared in front of the crowd and began acting out the divine play. He carried a torch of fire in one hand and red, black, white, green, and yellow streamers in the other, strode dramatically to one side of the stage where he handed them away.

His beauty was dazzling, he wore a beaded vest, jeans and a brilliant colored shirt of satin with ribbons at the shoulders. It was like he came down from a rainbow, the people said afterwards.

His dance with an old mother from the crowd who had no speaking part symbolized his bindings to the Earth. Yet, he told them, new rituals and mythic stories will be produced to respond to ecological, social, and economic changes and disasters. He held an eagle wing above his head as the old mother stepped solemnly to the beat of the drum.

Other figures wearing a variety of costumes, with offerings corresponding to rites and invocations no one had ever heard before, stood still on the concrete steps and told the oldest and newest stories, changed known and unfamiliar hymns, suggested the possibilities of their own sacrifices.

Some stories were known by everyone:
       I was not hostile to the white man. We had
       buffalo for food and their hides for clothing, and we

preferred the chase to a life of idleness and the
bickerings and jealousies, as well as the frequent periods of
starvation at the Agencies. But the grey fox came out in the
snow and bitter cold and destroyed my village. All of us would
have perished of exposure and hunger had we not recaptured
our ponies. Then Long Hair came in the same way.
They say we massacred him, but he would have
massacred us had we not defended ourselves and
fought to the death.

Some songs had always been sung:
The Sun, the light of the world,
I hear him coming.
I see His face as He comes.
He makes the beings on earth happy.
And they rejoice.
O Wakan-Tanka, I offer to you this world of light.

Most of those who represented a god had learned their parts perfectly
and told the others in the most convincing way that they would
collaborate with the sun, that they would listen to the songs and prayers
of the four grandmothers.

The domed building loomed in the background as a symbol of
colonialism and offered a realistic background for the long speeches by
the man in the beaded vest and another who joined him from the crowd.

The dialogue told of the valor of the two speakers, informed the others of
veiled intentions from evil ones, exhorted the people to "clear the way in a
sacred manner" and promised two things: "We shall be pierced by holy
men," and "We shall be told the stories."

Meanwhile, the brothers along with their cousins nearly faint from exhaustion and mental excitement became a part of the choir. They sang:

> "Who is the ghost over there?
> he tu we che ya e e
> Who is the ghost over there?
> he tu we che ya e e"

Even while the hymns, the songs of deep significance were still being composed and sung in the people's voices and the dances continued, the young male witnesses decided on the setting out: to go east in the manner of all young heroes in all myth.

They would follow the barren river to the place of the black and red colors, to the famous circle of dancers. The people would crowd about them again and the song would bring back to life the sacred trees. Their purpose would be to keep alive what everyone knew about tradition at a place made sacred again by their very presence.

It would be a journey of lamentation as well as pleasure on the road from oblivion to recovery, a human quest to give back the story.

VISITING PROFESSOR AND
THE YELLOW SKY

Yesterday afternoon
I woke and heard them again
raucous and loud
harsh in the dim sky,

the sleek crows trailing me into the southern
winds toward the warmth of the Bay
flapping above my window
angry and out of place
too large for these dainty trees

what do you think of crows, I ask
and without hesitation
answer
they belong up north
along the Platte
the Little Big Horn
the Cheyenne River
the creek named for them that swung past
my grandmother's house
along those mythical North Country
waters or the hills
of the west.

I know they have followed me here
but I don't know why
blue-black is the carnivore
yellow the sky.

I turned to the door and the
evening shade
and heard it differently

this time
it sounded like the drippings
from the hanging plant
I just watered

instead it was a moth
stuck between folded papers

blue-black is the carnivore
yellow the sky.

WRITER'S CHOICES

I went to my library
this morning. Slattern
volumes leaning upon one another
waited.

A novel is
"an expression of discontent,"
Llosa said.

Mendacious inventions
of historians
played at fawning over me
and I was lulled by the gracelesss words.

I shook the ink from corners
of old wounds and a voice
coming out of nowhere
told me that recognition
originates in dreams
and poetry.

A POET'S BRIEF ADDRESS TO THE STUDENTS AND FACULTY UPON THE OCCASION OF BEING NAMED DISTINGUISHED ALUMNA

Theses and Arguments
everlasting debates of moral philosophy
called for but never lived out in
anything but inner consciousness
are forgotten by everyone alive
and never even known to the young.
Lacking the allure of a Miller's High Life
in the backseat of someone's
borrowed car, Theses and Arguments
like lonely jet streams outlined in the vast sky
of the creative imagination only in retrospect
answer the question, what am I doing here?
and why?

I spent four years here.
They changed my life.

But becoming a poet was
my own secret idea.
The unconnected roads in
the infertile sod of Immigrant Civics
and Algebra 10 needed maps
to trails the buffalo made. In my day,
land-grant fields were not meant to be
hotbeds of Cultural Diversity. The
students from Bolivia, needy Indians like me,

all studying to be Civil Engineers,
called me "Isabella".
"Marry me," they said. "Marry me, Isabella."
And we dealt endless cards from stacked decks
at the Campus Café by custom
climbing over barriers of tortuous
Jacks and Queens to try to remember
the little dusty towns we came from
the insurmountable bridges of
our people's histories. Our homelands.
Wrenched from the arms of an Indian family
how far it seemed then
to find the path.

I spent four years here.
They changed my life.

"Dear Upperclassman,"
the dean's letter invited.
"May we schedule an appointment?"
When your parents sent you here
they sent you on your way.
Be brave.
There was no talk of what was good.
Only where the jobs might be:
Cincinnatti. L.A. St. Paul.
As though by making this fabulous
gesture to someone else's past, I would lie down and
sleep in the shadow of a secular and technological
new world and never question when the sun went down
what art and ancestors had to do with it.

CATHER'S OEUVRE — *the Immigrant Story*
Written After a Night of Re-Reading O Pioneers!

Against the glare at my dark window
I see beyond the reflection into
the pose a snowy night leaves
draped on a wooden lawn chair, humped and smooth,
slouching elegantly across the seat. A late-night
conversationalist to interrupt one's reading. One
long white mound lying outstretched on the
armrest. Languid. Undisturbed. Like
a crystal ball which might tell the
difference between what is sensible and what is not.
Out of the white-dark glare a voice comes, saying that
god was on their side. I stop turning the pages.
Pages written by the eponymous white woman
whose point was: "the history of every
country begins in the heart of a man or woman."
It is the immigrant story. Different from
the indigenous one which says "the heart
of any country begins in the heart
of the Earth." My thoughts turn to the place
of the rivers and the wind she thinks of
now as vestigial, mere remnant, traces of a human past.

In later morning following a good night's sleep
I pick up my reading. The sun emerges
bright and warm. Dapples of dripping snow
from the roof's eaves resound and my night companion slumps.
Small frail arms puddle a forlorn blanket of snow and
I see that the fortune teller is in bad shape. Our night talk

ended, unsuspicious pages dampened by the
thaw recede and blur, the snowy night's leavings
as transient as the translations of humans who
often get the story wrong.

SURVIVAL

At night, startled by the
snowy owl who flees her
perch I waken to the
sharp sound of sleet against
the cedar tree above
the spring: improbable
songs by keepers of the
wind recede toward mountains,
vacant voices in the
rain holding to the sway
in our own modern world
of ghosts upon the land.

Discomposed in the wake
of a vicious winter
rain storm the cedar tree
above the spring recalls
the stages of its own
fallen needles. Yet, the
exact memory of a
doomed universe is
undecipherable,
surreal. Overcoming
my fear I rise to close
the window, streaked and wet;
the holy winds are sent
to remind me I am
transient, adverse, mortal.
The best I can do is

listen to this oldest
version of the story.

In the dawn light mountains
cradle the breath of the
cedar tree above the
spring, droplets taking their
places on peeled limbs like
dancers from an ancient
world, prelude to ritual.

In the sun I dry the cuttings
taken from the cedar
tree above the spring and
hold in precise regard
the sacred smudging of
limbs and hair, a tribal
art meticulously
restored in my night dreams.

ÉLAN

— a poem for the men and women who are the Big Foot (Sitanka) Memorial Riders of 1990 and, especially, for Arvol Looking Horse

Sometimes after the glare of sunrise
but before the moon shines
they ride the frozen wind
dance du 'ventre in killing snow;
he holds the broken heart of a grieving god
in elegaic memory, bears in his
gloved hand the sacred eaglestaff.
Courage! Il ne passeront pas!

Between the monasticism of
priesthood and the flaring love
of a warrior's ways, he
holds his whitened breath
and becomes heroic
to the nation he honors.

FLUTE MAKER'S STORY

For those on prairie hills who make the sounds,
enrobe themselves in winter, cedar-bark;
they know the mythic pulse will part
the patterned prose of men who found
their origins in guise and art.
They play the flute and etch inflections of the heart
on sacred ground; the passing winters keep it thus.

Know it was always so that men who cast
and shape the reeds on hills remorselessly
will watch you wave your shawl yet interleaf,
mnemonically, the shadows of the past
with standard lines of life and grief.
They teach the word and song of old belief
forever in Maka', no magic sets you free.

DEER AT THE
KESHENA AMPHITHEATRE, 1993

The singers come from everywhere. Fine white
mists rise to shroud the Woodland Bowl; womblike,
deep and sacred, a place where rocks once
cleansed the spirit, it serves now
to hold hundreds of dancers in flimsy
light; it shares the scent of firs
and reeds that grow in wooded lands
known by the Menominee Chiefs of any age: Summer
Cloud. Lead Rabbit. Standing Behind. And Deer.
Scabby Robe from Montana shares the *cipelo*
songs of the Lakota. By invitation San Carlos
Crown Dancers, fickle and chalky, teasing, curing,
they dramatize the good part and the light. Bright, giddy
young shawl dancers and heavy, reposing old
women step in time, perfect, nimble. One sits still.
At last the woman in a red cotton powwow dress,
a dogged fighter, Bitch-Mother to the Tribes,
desperate daughter and Star Girl, dominates
the circle.
"You should know," her silence broken,
"that forty years ago my tribe, the Menominee
was terminated; twenty years later we were
restored; and today I come before you
as a true survivor of Indian Policy."
The dancers will leave
the womb tonight. And the
woman in red will turn
her face to the East. But not before

we look up to pray, calling and asking
that the mysteries, rulers of the day space even now,
be invoked. In that way we know
where it is safe to walk.

THIS IS THE ROAD

I first left on
scenic and coruscating
but straight as far
as the eye can see
edges cracked like egg shells
past little towns that seek some
common denominator for
a hundred years of predicting
I'd never come back.
Signs on abandoned motels
do nothing to control the predators.
The only travellers on this
road drive vans
with suitcases tied to their
tops moving away
from the swollen river
failed pick-ups in the crossroads
dance in the sun to the sway
of half-dead cottonwoods.
This is the road
I first left on
layers of clouds
rise in the sky
as far as the eye can see
dark and light there
grey and white
crowding about the feast
that is this earth
full, close enough to touch
mallards nesting beside it.

MASQUERADE

After decades of wearing the veiled mask
coming back to see the start of winter again
icy wind and stark snow the same white
noisy hawks riding waves in chilled flight
above the timbered slopes and wet hills
almost there, almost home
sounds in the treasured silence
of familial gratitude
welcome outstretched hands
again and again grasping the new day's
resolve of translating no more
the fateful script.

NOTES

Funeral Sermon

* In Dakota mythology, the stars around what the Europeans call the constellation Gemini make up a constellation the Dakotas call "the bear's home" and they disappear according to season. Dakotas depend upon the stability inherent in the star universe. Its loss is the end of fertility and growth.

Spider as She Used to Be

* Reference to an old traditional Dakota story told to the poet by her father, a Sisseton Dakota Indian born at Old Agency.
† An incident recorded in the South Dakota Department of History collections, Vol. XXIX.

The Last Remarkable Man

* An ancestor: hunka lowanpi is a rite of the Lakotas and it is called "the making of relatives." It is little understood and is misused, they say, in contemporary times.

Jesus Saves or Don't Ask Me to Join AA . . .

This poem is written in English as a villanelle, a French poetic form. It refers to a Lakota poetic form, the "forty-nine" which is a contemporary art form popular among young people. It is sung, usually to the accompaniment of a hand drum, at intertribal powwows, afterhours. The "forty-nine" is a drinking song, a social song, casual and extemporaneous. It often expresses humorous or absurd themes not meant to be serious though sometimes they are.

The Bleak Truth Is

This is a poem dedicated to Louie Andrew's father, a Spokane Indian, and my grandfather, a Dakotah. It is based upon an origin story first told to me by my grandfather. I heard a version of it thirty years later when I lived on the Spokane Indian Reservation and was surprised to discover that it was a story told for the same reasons, to know the forces in the universe and how the world was made.

The Flute Makers Story

* "Maka" means "the earth."

Elizabeth Cook-Lynn is a teacher, essayist, fiction writer and poet. A member of the Crow Creek Sioux Tribe, she was born on the reservation at Fort Thompson, South Dakota, in 1930. From 1971 until 1991 she taught English and Native American Studies at Eastern Washington University, before returning to live in South Dakota and write full-time. She is the author of *The Power of Horses*, (Short Stories, Arcade, 1990), *From the River's Edge*, (Novel, Arcade 1991), *Why I Can't Read Wallace Stegner*, (Essays, U. of Wisconsin, 1996), and most recently, co-written with Mario Gonzalez, *The Politics of Hallowed Ground: Wounded Knee and the Struggle for Indian Sovereignty*, (University of Illinois, 1998).